C000150651

1 MONTH OF
FREE
READING

at

www.ForgottenBooks.com

By purchasing this book you are eligible for one month membership to ForgottenBooks.com, giving you unlimited access to our entire collection of over 1,000,000 titles via our web site and mobile apps.

To claim your free month visit:

www.forgottenbooks.com/free191022

* Offer is valid for 45 days from date of purchase. Terms and conditions apply.

ISBN 978-0-484-40102-9
PIBN 10191022

This book is a reproduction of an important historical work. Forgotten Books uses
state-of-the-art technology to digitally reconstruct the work, preserving the original format
whilst repairing imperfections present in the aged copy. In rare cases, an imperfection in
the original, such as a blemish or missing page, may be replicated in our edition. We do,
however, repair the vast majority of imperfections successfully; any imperfections that
remain are intentionally left to preserve the state of such historical works.

Forgotten Books is a registered trademark of FB &c Ltd.
Copyright © 2018 FB &c Ltd.
FB &c Ltd, Dalton House, 60 Windsor Avenue, London, SW19 2RR.
Company number 08720141. Registered in England and Wales.

For support please visit www.forgottenbooks.com

THE

COMMONWEALTH

OF

REASON.

WRITTEN BY

WILLIAM HODGSON, ESQ.

WHO WAS CONFINED TWO YEARS IN NEWGATE ON A
CHARGE OF SEDITION.

The Privileged Orders may pass away, but the People will be eternal.
Mirabaud.

Liberty is the Right and Happiness of all, for all by Nature are Equal
and Free, and no one can, without the utmost injustice, become the Slave
of his like.—*Inscription on the Athenian Statue of Liberty.*

London :

PRINTED AND PUBLISHED BY THOMAS DAVISON,
10, DUKE STREET, WEST SMITHFIELD.

1820.
Price One Shilling.

Hox
1820

ADVERTISEMENT.

THE Publisher of this little work having been solicited to bring out an impression on a more reasonable scale than the three *former Editions*, did not feel himself justified in proceeding, till he had made every enquiry relative to the wishes of the Author; but after a fruitless research of many months for that highly-valuable man, he has been urged to produce it at the present price, **by** *Mr. Hodgson's* friends, as, from his known goodness of heart, and philanthropic disposition, he would feel happy in a wider dissemination of this matchless production.

The Publisher has to hope, that should this *Ad-vertisement ever meet the eye* of *Mr. Hodgson*, he will not for a moment entertain or attribute any sordid or selfish motives to him, for he is very willing, and it is his intention, to devote the profits (after the expences of publishing, &c. are de-frayed) to some political object.

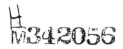
M342056

PREFACE.

As the end of all government is, or ought to be, the security, happiness, and advantage of the governed, and not the exclusive benefit and interest of those intrusted with the legislative or executive power, who should only be considered as the organs by which the majority of the community express their will, and as the servants of the Commonwealth, amenable at all times, for their conduct to the *people*, these being the fountain from whence *alone* can spring *legitimate authority;* it may not be unacceptable, in these *speculative times,* when the science of political government appears to have awakened men's curiosity in an extraordinary degree, and the greater part of the world seem bent on the investigation of its principles, and on the destruction of those *abuses*, the existence of which has but too long disgraced civilized society, to have some mode pointed out, by which, should any of the present systems, so fraught with ruin, and injurious to the true interests of mankind, be abolished, we can reasonably hope to obtain what ought to constitute the only object of every institution, whether political or social—*public happiness,* from which source alone can flow individual felicity.

For this desirable purpose, the following Plan for *a Commonwealth, to be founded on the broad and durable basis of reason, liberty, fraternity, and equality,* is submitted to the candid consideration and impartial examination of mankind. If, by the publication of it, the author shall .

be instrumental in removing any single grievance, out of
the enormous and almost countless number under which
men at present labour, no matter in what part of nature's
wide-extended empire, he will consider his efforts as amply
and honourably rewarded. If, on the contrary, it shall not be
found to yield an idea, by which the present *miserable* and
unhappy condition of man can be ameliorated, he shall
console himself with the pleasurable reflection that must
necessarily result from a conviction, that although his judg-
ment may have erred, his intentions were honest, sincere,
and well-meant; and he will retire, without experiencing
any other painful sensation, than that of wanting the ability
to do good, into that obscurity from which he never wishes
to emanate, but for the purpose of increasing the prosperity
and happiness of his fellow-creatures, and which he conceives
he can never do more effectually than by pointing out to them
the *truth,* and entreating them on every occasion to consult
their *reason* and their *experience.*

CONTENTS.

THE

COMMONWEALTH

OF

REASON.

To be completed in Twelve Weekly Numbers.

FIRST PUBLISHED IN 1795.

EXPERIENCE having proved *corruption* to be the most
dreadful evil that can possibly affect either public or private
life, it is of course that which men should be most studious
to avoid ; any endeavour, therefore, to raise up barriers
against this all-destructive vice, may be considered as one of
the noblest efforts of the human understanding :—as from
thence has proceeded all those arbitrary and diabolical actions
we have at different periods witnessed : and of which such
innumerable examples, that have justly called down the exe-
cration of mankind, are furnished in the history of the
world.

As corruption is generally the result of power long con-
tinued in the same individual, and prevention more humane
and far better than detection, it is a desire in this little work
to make every situation in the Commonwealth, to which is
attached either trust or power,—REVOLUTIONARY or ROTA-
TIVE; thereby taking this best remedy for, and precaution
against, this most inveterate enemy to public happiness.—
this epidemic that has hitherto baffled the most strenuous
efforts of the most able physicians,—this political Upas,*
under whose baneful and malignant branches every virtue
finds immediate death.

Philosophers must long since have been convinced that the
abuse of power is much more the consequence of long and
uninterrupted possession in the hands of individuals, than
of any other cause whatever : and as it is an axiom in poli-
tics, " *that wherever there is power, there will be abuse,*"
it is but right to imagine, that by making the power neces-

* The name of a poison-tree in Java.

1

sarily vested in a part to be exercised for the benefit of the
whole, as fleeting, and of as little duration as possible, in the
same individual, we obviate the great *error* in political institutions, which seems to be a delegation of those powers, to
be exercised without a just control, and for a long and some-
times for an indefinite space of time, that requires the eyes
of an Argus, and a frequent change of persons to prevent
them from degenerating (by corruption) into tyranny and
oppression.

As *pretended distinctions* amongst men, *who are all
equal by nature*, and are all, unquestionably, equally help-
less in infancy, and equally cold in the embraces of death,
have a tendency to create a difference of interests in the
same community, in which the weaker is invariably swal-
lowed up, and destroyed by the stronger; and human beings,
otherwise naturally friends and brothers, are thereby set at
enmity with each other, for the enjoyment of paltry titles,
that do not *really* distinguish the possessors from the mass
of mankind, except in particular and local situations.

This Plan will propose that no grade, or title of distinction
whatever, shall exist among the citizens of the Commonwealth, except what the exercise of superior benevolence
and virtue shall obtain from the general respect of society,
or what the *temporary* possession of the public functions
shall necessarily demand for the moment. Thus all being
citizens, equal in rights, none will have an interest separate
from that of his neighbour, since no one will be capable of
infringing or invading the right of another, without involving
not only his own, but that of the whole Commonwealth, of
which he himself makes an integral part; of course every
such attempt will, in this state of perfect equality, be re-
sisted not only by the citizen attacked, but by the collective
force of the whole community, whose direct interest will effectually point out the absolute necessity of the opposition :
whilst daily experience teaches us to know, that in those
states where an inequality of rights does exist, it frequently
becomes the interest and desire of one class to subvert and
destroy the rights of another class, thereby, as they falsely
conceive, the more effectually to establish and support what
the errors of their constitution have led them to consider
as their own. Thus, in such states, it very rarely, or never
happens, that the collective body of the citizens find an occasion, where their common interest is united. On this
principle we may account for the fall of those vast and

mighty empires which history informs us *once had existence,*[*] and of which we have not now a single vestige left, whereby to descry their ancient power and grandeur, except the traditionary detail handed down to us by our ancestors; for it is an old proverb in England, the truth of which has been universally admitted,—" THAT A HOUSE DIVIDED AGAINST ITSELF, CANNOT STAND." As the accumulation of immense wealth in the hands of individuals, by any other means than personal industry, or equitable inheritance, may with great truth be considered as the primary and most effectual means by which the fiend—CORRUPTION, secretly undermines, and finally overturns the best and wisest institutions; the endeavour to destroy this channel of abuse, this panacea, that infallibly turns all virtue into vice, without rendering injustice to any one, is surely highly deserving the consideration and attention of mankind; and as such will form a part of the Plan. Seeing, therefore, that *entailed estates*, and laws of *primogeniltureship*, and other unequal and unjust decrees, respecting the distribution of property, are the *causes* of these mischievous masses of wealth, so highly dangerous to, and incompatible with, the existence of LIBERTY, and which have been always found to furnish the ready means of CORRUPTION, OPPRESSION, and TYRANNY, the only alteration required will be, that in no possible case shall the different children, whether male or female, of the same father, divide in other than equal portions, the property of which the sire may die possessed. Thus we shall prevent that disgraceful inequality of patrimony in children of the same parent, that at present furnish not unfrequent instances, where the head of the family, as he is called, has a revenue of, perhaps, *forty thousand pounds a year*, whilst the younger branches have scarcely a sufficient income to support the appearance that custom has rendered absolutely necessary to enable them to dine at their elder brother's table; to provide for whom, without injuring the possessions of the elder son, an almost incredible number of *sinecure places*, and of trifling and useless offices, have been created under the different governments the world has hitherto witnessed; the burthen of which has, without exception,

---

[*] It is the Publisher's intention of presenting the English Nation with a work in cheap numbers, giving a detailed account of the Fall of those Empires, and every circumstance connected with their Rise and Decline.

ultimately fallen on those, who, it must ever be acknowledged, form the great bulwark of every state—THE IN-
DUSTRIOUS ARTIZAN AND LABOURIOUS CULTIVATOR,—
as the payment of these places is usually provided for by
taxes levied on articles of the most general consumption, and
of the first necessity:—independent of which, these rich men
become themselves the *servile tools*, and *abject slaves* of
the executive power; as upon no other condition can they
reasonably hope to make provision for their poorer relatives.
Thus the only return the citizens receive for encouraging
this immoral and partial distribution of the father's estate,
is the deprivation of the independent assistance of those
whom, by the most flagrant injustice, they have loaded with
riches. For these reasons it will be advisable not to admit
in the Commonwealth of any *sinecure place*, than the existence of which nothing can be more absurd: for no one
can consistently with honesty, accept of payment for services he has never performed, nor has the remotest intention of performing. And when these fellows are inter-
rogated as to their *nobility*, they turn round with an
unparralleled degree of effrontery, and assert that it is an
" *indecent attack upon the king's* LAWFUL *prerogative* * ."
In fact, SINECURE PLACES MAY BE LITERALLY
DENOMINATED—*A ROBBERY COMMITTED ON
THE NATION, UNDER THE FALSE COLORS,
AND SPECIOUS PRETEXT, OF HAVING A PUBLIC
EMPLOYMENT ;*—and the existence and duration of
such emoluments can only be built on the disgraceful ignorance and culpable inattention of the greater part of the
citizens composing the Commonwealth;—since no man in
his senses would, knowingly, pay his baker for a loaf he
never had, or was to have. Neither is it necessary to suffer
the establishment of any useless office, or employment in the
Commonwealth, which can only be harassing to the citizens

---

* Suppose Charles George Arden should be asked why he is more
particularly entitled to £38,574, than any other individual;—or
Lord Cathcart to £27,864;—or Francis Rawdon Hastings to £26,000;
—or Francis Gerard Lake to £12,649;—or the Earl of Talbot to
£20,000; they will tell you it is " an indecent attack upon the
king's prerogative." In fact, should we enquire of the 2,344 Pensioners' and Sinecurists, why they collectively receive £2,474,805,
they will furnish you with the same answer, no doubt. In Great
Britain alone there has been a calculation made that the Sinecurists
and Pensioners deprive of sustenance no less a number of individuals
than 381,525.

and destructive to their common interest Or to admit any enormous or disproportionate salary to be annexed, to the execution of the necessary public functions; for as no citizen ought to refuse to take upon him, in his turn, that public employment, which a majority, of his fellow-citizens shall call him to the exercise of,—and as the due, faithful, and impartial discharge of it is as much for his own security, happiness, and advantage, as for that of the Commonwealth, so no citizen who really wishes to promote the general prosperity of the Commonwealth, can or ought to have a desire of *wickedly* enriching himself at the expense of the community; which he certainly does whenever he accepts, as a remuneration for his public services, a sum greater than will defray the necessary expenses and consumption of time that has attended them, or of a sinecure, or of a pension, or of a place of profit, the functions of which produce no general good to the citizens.   Therefore, not suffering any of these places or profits, *the existence of which, in the governments we have hitherto witnessed, may be justly stiled "a radical error,"* is the best and most certain way to prevent the dreadful necessity of *reforming, abuses,* that we ourselves are the authors of, by permitting such temptations to be thrown in the way of the evil-disposed, avaricious, and designing men:—for as it is an axiom in metaphysics, *" that no effect can possibly exist without a cause,"* so it is also an axiom in medicine, *" that if you can remove the cause, the effect will cease."*

As the existence of *exclusive privileges* is the grand means by which these unhappy jealousies, shameful dissentions, and destructive animosities, that have ever been found to be absolutely necessary to the support and existence of *arbitrary oppression, despotic power,* and *lawless corruption,* are fomented and kept alive, and which effectually prevent that harmony that ought ever to subsist among the members of the Commonwealth; it must appear evident to every thinking and reasonable being, that those customs which have no other tendency than to destroy the happy union of interests so requisite to the furtherance of the happiness and prosperity of the citizens, could only have originated with those monsters, (for they are a disgrace to the name of man,) who, lost to every social virtue, and wishing to trample with impunity on the *sacred* and *indefeasible rights of man,* have cunningly introduced a system of OPPRESSING ONE MAN FOR THE PROFIT OF ANOTHER, which, from the extreme ignorance of mankind and their but too general inattention to their true and genuine interests, they have been able to pass on their blindness and credulity, as favors and advantages;—and who, by these nefarious means, having acquired the direction of the public force, have, whenever the *cheat* has been discovered, *and men have attempted to regain their original state of happy equality*, made use of that command thus surreptitiously obtained, to perpetuate a system, by which alone such MISCREANTS and VIOLATERS OF JUSTICE, knew they could be enabled to commence with safety, and continue with impunity, their diabolical measures, enormous speculations, and sanguinary administration. For these reasons, I propose, that in my Plan no such heterogeneous and corrupt monsters of injustice, as PRIVILEGED ORDERS, GAME LAWS, MANORIAL RIGHTS, EXCLUSIVE CHARTERS, CORPORATIONS, and OTHER SUCH PARTIAL, WICKED, and OPPRESSIVE PRIVILEGES shall have existence : for nothing seems more irrational, than that the birds of the air, wild animals, or the fish of a river, which nature certainly has not stamped or marked with any particular man's name, and to which no one man can justly and honestly shew a superior claim over his neighbour, should be made the exclusive property of the rich man, and the poor man be punished for the killing and appropriation of that which nature seems to have sent for the express purpose of appeasing those appetites she has given him in common with the most wealthy and affluent. And it can never, surely, be argued, that the destroying of these creatures is in itself an immoral act ; as, supposing such argument to be just, it could not but be admitted at the same time, that if it is immoral in the man of poverty, it is equally so in the man of riches : unless, indeed, men can be so weak and stupid as to imagine, that a rich man, lord of the manor, or other privileged person, has a licence and authority from Heaven, which purges the guilt from him, that attaches on the poor man's shoulders : and yet, ridiculous as this supposition must appear to every man of common sense, we nevertheless hear of some men whose infallibility is accredited, and even held sacred, with a great part of the world : which acknowledgment, on their parts, is absolutely supposing the existence of this monstrous and incomprehensible absurdity. Neither can anything be more ridiculous, cruel, and unjust, than that A should have a remedy against his neighbour B, that B has not in like cases against his brother citizen A, since what is punishable when done by B, can or ought to be no less so when committed by A, however ignorant men, by absurd and nonsensical privileges, ac corded to A, may have sheltered him from common justice' and enabled, and indeed encouraged him to commit, without fear of inquiry, or punishment, those acts of dishonesty and oppression to B, for which, but strip him of his talismanic garments, he would be held in utter and general detestation.

As what are called, *national religious establishments*, have been found to be the greatest scourge that ever afflicted mankind; and have, at different periods, been perverted from what even the original institutors themselves meant should be their object; and have been called into the aid of, incorporated with, and made part of almost every national government, by which means *corruption* has engendered, at the moderate expence of a few mitres and other such baubles, an additional and most implacable enemy to the natural independence of man: and have by instilling the monstrous and incongruous doctrine of eternal damnation to such as differ in opinion from the national theology, robbed a great part of the citizens of their *just, necessary* and *inde- feasible rights,* under the specious, and diabolical pretence of heterodoxy; and compelled the inhabitants of one coun- try, to murder the citizens of another, for the propagation of what, *each has called the true religion,* to their mutual dis- advantage, and in direct defiance of the morality inculcated by all;—one of the great and principal tenets of these reli- gion-mongers, being, according to their language, though not according to their practice, *to promote brotherhood and good-will amongst men;* yet, how far this principle actuates those who call themselves orthodox, *which each does in his turn,* may be best collected from the reciprocal benevolence they exercise towards each other; from a Jew being con- demned to the *Auto-de-Fe* in Spain and Portugal, because he will not believe that Jesus Christ was the son of God; from a Christian being held in general abhorrence by the Turks, because he doubts the truth of Mahomet's having ascended seven Heavens, and held converse with the Al- mighty; from a Roman Catholic being prevented in Pro- testant countries holding any public office or place of trust and profit; merely because he believes the wine and the wafer he receives when taking the sacrament, is the body and blood of his friend Jesus Christ, whilst the true be- liever, as he is stiled, under what the persecuted Catholic calls an heretical government, says, they are only taken in remem- brance of their Lord and Master; betwixt whom and his present followers, there is no more resemblance, "than I to

Hercules;"—and a thousand other wicked and diabolical pains and penalties attached to the great, enormous, and never-to-be-forgiven crime of a man's thinking and judging for himself, in what is called the most material concern of his life, the salvation of his soul; not to mention the cruel and murderous wars that have been carried on by Jews against Gentiles; Christians against Turks; Turks against Infidels; and one sect of Christians against another sect of Christians; in which barbarous, bloody, and blasphemous contests, millions of infatuated men have lost their lives, without the point in dispute being yet-determined; the com batants having been always reduced to the situation of the hare and the bound :—*where one was too fatigued to follow, and the other too tired to run away;* therefore, as every establishment in a Commonwealth should be really and truly to promote *fraternity* among the citizens, and to draw closely the bonds of union in society; it follows of course, that these institutions, experience having proved them to be productive of contrary effects, should by every well wisher and friend to the repose and happiness of mankind be avoided. And as religion seems to be a subject on which men may perhaps never be perfectly agreed; since no one can, by any thing like demonstrative evidence, prove that the tenets of the particular sect to which he belongs, is more acceptable to the Supreme Being, than those of another sect, whether he be Baptist, Jew, Gentile, Mahometan, Armenian, Christian, Antichristian, Adamite, Dunker, Swedenborgian, Worshipper of the Sun, Worshipper of the Moon, Universalist, Eutychian, Adrammelechian, Philadelphian, Quartodecimanian, Predestinarian, Agonyclite, Bonasian, Basilidian, Hottentot, Nestorian, Carpocratian, Antinomian, Maronist, Cartesian, Scotist, Thomist, Scripturist, Sacramentarian, Worshipper of Fo, Gnostic, Idolator, Quietest, Sabattarian, Manichean, Roman Catholic, Trinitarian, Anti-trinitarian, Rhetorian, Mengrelian, Annomæan, Brownist, Whitfieldite, Cataphrygian, Messalian, Pelagian, Semipelagian, Elcesacitian, Anthropomorphite, Millenarian, Antidicomarionite, Cerdonist, Elaterist, Stercorauist, Jacobite, Georgian, Antitactite, Congregationalist, Collutbean, Berulian, Eudoxian, Solifidian, Priscillianist, Melchite, Herodian, Cerinthian, Appollinarian, Agynite, Papist, Quintillian, Sceptic. Circumcellian; Disciplinarian, Eunomian, Albongist, Metemsychite, Lollard, Hemerobaptist, Fratricellian, Archontick, Eternalist, Dissenter, Samaritan, Remonstrant. Opinionist, Patripassiant, Artolyrist, Aquarian, Ubiquitarian, Photinjan, Marianalatrist,

Sublapsarian, Supralapsarian, Metamorphist, Ebionite, Jansenist, Rogatist, Mennonite, Sabean, Apellitian, Marcionist, Dulcinist, Catharian, Ascordrigilian, Macedonian, Augustinian, Montanist, Chiliast, Muncerian, Libertine, Bongomilian, Rebaptizer, Bardesanist, Severian, Gentoo, Barulite, Apostolian, Bacchanalian, Arian, Sabellian, Quaker, Bagnolensian, Pharisee, Vaudois, Erastian, Petrobrusian, Timothean, Luciferian, Baanite, Eustathian, Flagellant, Monotheist, Socinian, Tritheite, Stoic, Gortinian, Sofee, Braman, Sethian, Faster, Protestant, Sandemonian, Lutheran, Calvinist, Fifthmonarchist, Seleucian, New Jerusalemite, Polygamist, Fatalist, Polytheist, Nazarite, Gaulonite, Florinusite, Sabathian, Valentinian, Jovinianist, Sadducee, Pyrrhonist, Pythagorean, Presbyterian, Methodist, Optimist, Donatist, Moravian, Muggletonian, Deist, Novatian, Tao-sse, Unitarian;—it follows, of course, that setting up one species of religion in preference to others, or nationalizing it, by countenancing, protecting, and supporting in idleness and luxury such drones as Muftis, Popes, Ta-ho-changs, Great Lamas, Parsons, Archbishops, Deaconesses, Rectors, High-Priests, Elders, Fakirs, Bishops, Deacons, Mustaphas, Archdeacons, Druids, Priestesses, Levites, Priors, Canons, Deans, Priests, Doctors of Divinity, Ho-changs, Nuns, Rabbies, Monks, Abbés, Carmelites, Jesuits, Carthusians, Dominicans, Franciscans, Lady Abbesses, Masorites, Lamas, Cardinals, Emirs, Vicars, Prophets, Prebends, Talapolins, Bonzes, Bramins, Apostles, Seers, Primontres, Benedictines, Jacobines, Feuillans, Bernardines, Freres de l'Ordre de la Mercy, Cordeliers, Capuchins, Recollects, Freres de la Charité, Minimes, Oratorians, Chartreux, Predicateurs, Picpuces, Carmes, Augustines, Ursulines, Calverians, Clerines, Sœurs de la Croix, Barnabites, Sœurs de la Charite, Annonciats, Sœurs de St. Thomas, Carmes de Chaussée, Petit Peres, Dames de St. Claire, Lazarists, Ordre de St. Benoit, Dames de la Visitation, Celestines, Chapitre, Nobles des Femmes, Chanoins, Trapistes, Incas, Friars, Curates, Clergymen, Chaplains, and other such useless beings, or *as they emphatically style each other*, IMPUDENT IMPOSTORS, who being too proud and lazy to work, have availed themselves of man's credulity, and the corruption of the executive power, to get laws enacted, enabling them to steal with impunity from the laborious and industrious citizens; and who, not content with thus cheating mankind, have contrived to defraud each other in the division of the spoil, by giving to one, because he wears a cap of a

2

particular form, and of his own invention, TEN OR TWELVE THOUSAND POUNDS A YEAR; whilst the poor devils who read all their tenets to the infatuated multitude are allowed by these *meek, moderate, temperate, sober, honest, chaste, virtuous, modest, dignified,* and *superior* interpreters of what, *as they say of each other,* each impiously chooses to call God's holy word, perhaps FIFTEEN OR TWENTY POUNDS A YEAR; but then their motto is *patience, and perhaps I may be a cardinal, bishop, pope, mufti, Ta-ho-chang, Great Lama, or high-priest;* it follows, I say, that these establishments, which produce such caterpillars, who pretend that an all just God has sent them to devour the good things of this world, without contributing to the labour of producing them, can be attended with no other consequence than that unhappy one of exciting the most rancorous animosities and implacable resentments betwixt those whose immediate interest consists in preserving the utmost cordiality, harmony, and fraternity, with each other, because they are at every instant endeavouring to gain superiority the one over the other, by engendering the most vicious hatred in their followers against all who happen to dissent from their particular doctrine ; I therefore propose, as religion is a subject merely of opinion, and consequently ought to be free as the circumambient air, not to suffer the building, at other than private expence, any *cathedral, mosque, synagogue, convent, pagoda, church, monastery, tabernacle, conventicle, abbey, meeting-house, nunnery, pantheon, chapel, temple, altar,* or other edifice, to be appropriated to the purpose of what is called NATIONAL RELIGIOUS WORSHIP ; or the endowment of any MONASTERY or NUNNERY; or the existence of any tythes, or other provision for what are called the REGULAR and NATIONAL CLERGY; taking it for granted, that the citizens can never be more happy, or the Commonwealth more flourishing, than when they follow that precept in ethics, of *" Do unto all men as you would they should do unto you;"* which great and immutable principle of morality is invaded, whenever one man attempts to deprive another of any of his rights, merely because he happens to differ from him in religious opinions ; for who will say, that the Swede, when he castrates the deluded Roman Catholic priest, who has the misfortune to be found in his country, would not think himself ill used by being served in the same manner, whenever he chanced to go to Rome ; and nevertheless this is one of those savage customs, amongst a prodigious number of others, equally barbarous, that have been introduced by these religionists, who, with unblushing effrontery and unparalleled impudence, tell you, that in so doing they zealously serve the Supreme Being, promote the happiness of man, and propagate the doctrines of that great and good man, Jesus Christ, of whom it is recorded, in the New Testament, a book which these hypocrites themselves pretend to believe the truth of, that he was of so meek a disposition, that, in his advice to his disciples and followers, he said, *"If any man smite thee on the right cheek, turn to him the left also."*

And as the establishment of laws, however good and wholesome they may be, can be of no real use or service to the citizens, whilst the most effectual care is not taken to obtain a fair, impartial, and speedy execution of them; and as all experience must have long since convinced men that suffering of the law to be practised by individuals, for their own peculiar benefit and advantage, thereby making a trade of that which should form a principal and prominent feature in the executive power of the Commonwealth, is a principle that is radically founded in error, militates directly against a due and equitable administration of justice, is attended with the most injurious consequences to society; with the most melancholy examples of ruin and poverty to the parties seeking redress, and above all, has become, in the hands of COR-RUPTION, a very principal means of enslaving nations, of destroying the great and sacred rights of man, and of rending asunder those fraternal bonds, which should ever unite the citizens in the most brotherly affection to each other; and the laws having, in most countries, under the most flimsy pretext and specious assertion of maintaining peace, order, and good government, of every one of which they are at present entirely subversive, no doubt, expressly with a view to the particular interests of those legal wolves, who are continually prowling in society, seeking whom they may devour, become so complicated and entangled, that a whole life spent in the most unremitting study of them, is not sufficient to ascertain, with precision, what is or is not law, whereby the great bulk of the citizens of most countries are left in ignorance, and the most shameful state of blindness, of what ought to constitute their principal instruction, namely, a clear and accurate knowledge of those laws under which they live, are governed, and by which their lives, fortunes, and honour, are liable every day to be judged; and as the present method of administering public justice in most countries is such, that the greater part of the citizens are imbued with a belief that they have no occasion to obtain a knowledge of the laws of their nation, since they can always be able to find men who have studied them in a manner that is termed *professional,* and these, to keep up the delusion and error, purposely contrive to render them so intricate and perplexing, that the generality of men are deterred from entering upon an examination of their principles, and, by this trick, the public justice of a country is held up to sale like goods at an auction, where the best bidder generally is the purchaser, with this difference, that whereas in the auction, the buyer may perhaps be benefited by his bargain, the gainer of a law-suit is but too generally ruined, and in a worse condition than if he had quietly put up with the first injury ; indeed, the lawyers are, in fact, in almost all countries the most zealous, and strongest inculcators of Christianity ; for experience soon teaches all their clients, to their cost, that it is much more for their advantage to follow that precept of Jesus Christ, where he says, "And him that taketh away thy cloak forbid him not to take thy coat also, and of him that taketh away thy goods, ask them not again," than employ an attorney to recover them, for frequently in attempting to recover his hat, the citizen has the misfortune to lose his coat, waistcoat, shirt, stockings, and breeches ; it should seem, therefore, that those societies, which are established for the purpose of propagating the Christian Faith, would do well to recommend to the Pope the supplying all vacant church establishments with these strenuous supporters of the doctrines of Jesus Christ, instead of those clergymen, who, by their conduct, seem determined rather to bring Christianity into disesteem than promote its interests; and as distributive justice demands that every where the laws ought really to be what the English judges say the law of their country is, equally open to the poor and the rich ; although how far this is the case in most countries may be best judged of by the daily occurrences, where, if a man have not wherewith to fee an avaricious attorney, his complaints, however just, against his neighbour, must remain unheard and unredressed, whilst there are not wanting abundance of instances, where the man of wealth, by the mere dint of money, *properly applied, as the men of law professionally term it,* has been able to harass, oppress, and ruin his fellow-citizen, without any just cause whatever ; and to what is all this to be attributed, but that which is considered by the profession as their sheet anchor, and emphatically termed the *glorious uncertainty of the law,* which rendered into plain English, is, *whose attorney is the greatest rogue, who has the longest purse, and the most convenient witnesses ;* and as this glorious uncertainty of the law, so much valued and boasted of by its professors, is, or ought to be, its greatest reproach, because the law should equally apply to all the citizens, and none be suffered to be ignorant of it ; should be definite, and never be so made as to admit of two or more constructions ; and as delay in the determination of causes, is of all things the most destructive of justice, by opening a wide and extensive field for corruption, perjury, and oppression, and is highly harassing, and cruel to the parties accused ; their being a variety of examples where citizens who were extremely innocent of the crime alledged, have been detained in prison for six, nine, twelve months, and more, without being ever brought to trial, and at last discharged without any thing like evidence being offered of their guilt ; therefore, to remedy these evils, I propose, in my plan, not to suffer any attorney or advocate to be paid at the private expence of the individual seeking justice, but propose, that the law, the just and equitable administration of which is a circumstance mutually interesting to the whole body of the citizens, should really be what the administrators of English jurisprudence say of their laws, equally attainable by the affluent and the needy, and for this purpose, I propose, that it should at all times be administered at public expence, and without any unnecessary delay ; thus preventing any useless and inconvenient disbursement of money on the part of either plaintiff or defendant, and giving every citizen his remedy against oppression ; thus restoring Justice to her original purity, by taking out of her beam that bias which at present but too often causes one of her scales to preponderate, and never permitting her sword to strike but when truth directs the blow.

PLAN, &c.

- I SHALL now proceed to lay down the outlines of my plan for a COMMONWEALTH, and here I must entreat the candid reader to bear in mind, that if any part or the whole of it, may appear incongruous, I shall feel the greatest pleasure in seeing my feeble attempts taken up by a more masterly hand, and that happiness, which is the undoubted right of, and which I most fervently wish my fellow creatures to possess, placed by superior abilities, within the reach of oppressed mortals, by the proposition for a rational Government, to be founded on the indefeasible rights of man,—the non-existence of which in most countries has hitherto so cruelly scourged the human species, sinking them in slavery, sloth, and baseness ; making them hug those chains they ought to rend asunder; corrupting their morals, degenerating their habits, and submitting them to the cruel and rapacious tyranny of a few crafty knaves and designing villains, that punish the imbecility of those who imitate their example with the most bloody and dreadful tortures ; thus filling their prisons with the wretched victims of their savage policy, or else strewing the earth with the dead and mangled carcases of those who, left destitute by the negligence of society, have been forced into criminal pursuits to obtain that provision which their physical wants have rendered absolutely necessary, but which the injustice and rapacity of these unfeeling gaolers of the human mind has prevented them from being capacitated to obtain by other means, than depredating in their turn upon those who never cease for an instant to pillage and ravage their fellow-citizens, to support themselves in the most shameful debauchery and extravagant dissipation ;—regardless of the misery and wretchedness which they everywhere diffuse by the gratification of those inordinate and desolating passions that reduce them in the eyes of the honest and virtuous man, far below the level of the beasts of the field. Indeed, government, in the most part of the present societies, may be compared to caterpillars and locusts, who destroy, without remorse, the produce of the industry and labour of others, without ever dreaming of giving, in any manner, their assistance in return.

I can truly say, that the endeavour to point out the means of establishing such a government has been the most prominent motive for the present publication; conscious of the deficiency of my own acquirements in the prosecution of this design, I can flatter myself with nothing more than the hope that I may by it excite in the bosom of the *philosopher* and man of reflection, the desire of ameliorating the miseries of his species; which, whatever may be the difference of opinion between men on the best means of remedying them, must at all events be universally acknowledged but too fatally to have existence, and to cry aloud for redress:' no man of humanity can look at the cottager, and see him meagre, half-famished, and worn down with excessive toil,— his children naked and uneducated,—and at the same time view the plumpness and healthy appearance of the coach-horse that drags his lord in enervating idleness past the humble thatch, and not be ready to allow, that wherever such a wicked disparity between the condition of the human and brutal species exists, the government must be radically wrong, infamous, and little calculated to produce the desirable end for which government was originally instituted.

To the critics, I can only say, I shall cheerfully submit to their lashes, while they inflict them only in conformity to justice and reason; and that, far from feeling myself angered by their animadversions, however severe they may be, I shall be happy in having my mistakes rectified, and to be drawn from my wanderings into the path of truth; to be imbued with those sublime doctrines, forms the most zealous wish of my heart; and to inculcate the fascinating, beautiful, and delicious tenets of this long-neglected though radiant sun of human felicity, bounds the utmost ambition of my soul; and should I ever again appear before the public tribunal, I shall feel it the most honourable part of my life, candidly to acknowledge my errors, and thankfully to recognize the benefits that I may have received from the impartial observations of the learned, and the honest criticisms of the friends of humanity and truth.

This premised, I think it proper and suitable to my subject, to set out with a Declaration of Rights, founded on the broad and permanent basis of *Liberty, Fraternity*, and

Equality, as I conceive it is on the imperishable foundation of these rights alone, that those laws and regulations can be built, which shall truly and faithfully have for object, what ought to be considered the most important of all human pursuits—*The happiness of the human race living together in society.*

DECLARATION OF RIGHTS.

ARTICLE I.—All men, when they come out of the hands of Nature, are equal and free. This freedom and equality they can never infringe without committing injustice to themselves; they ought always to remain equal and free: no distinction ought to exist amongst the citizens but what is conducive to the general utility and happiness of society; any privilege, therefore, granted to a member of society for his own particular advantage, becomes an injustice to the rest of the citizens.

ART. 2.—The legitimate end of all association whatever, is the conservation of society, and the preservation of the natural and imprescriptible rights of each of its members: these rights are Liberty, Security, and Resistance against Oppression of every kind, and are founded on the nature of man.

ART. 3.—The SOVEREIGNTY ought to reside in the majority of the citizens who compose a nation. No *body of men* of less amount than the absolute majority; no *individual*, unless authorised by a complete majority, can legitimately exercise any authority over the citizens, because Nature has willed that its part shall always remain subordinate to the whole.

ART. 4.—Liberty consists in the power of doing every thing for the advantage of the individual which does not trench upon the rights of another: thus no restriction ought to be laid on the rights of any man, because, whenever the exercise of a function becomes injurious to society, it ceases to be Liberty, and becomes *licentiousness;* but as every man may not be able to form to himself an accurate and precise idea of what constitutes Licentiousness, the law, which, to be just, must be the expression of the will of the absolute majority of the citizens, fixes boundaries to the actions of men. The true and sole limitation of Liberty is, the not doing that to another which you would not wish he should do unto you.

ART. 5.—The law can acquire no right to forbid those actions which are not injurious to society. Every thing that is not forbidden by the law, each citizen ought to be allowed to do with safety, and ought to be by the law guaranteed in doing; but no citizen ought to be obliged to do that which is not prescribed by the law made antecedent to the compulsion.

ART. 6.—The law ought to be the expression of the will of the majority of the citizens comprising a state; a majority of the citizens, by themselves or their representatives, ought to consent to the law before it can have effect: it ought to be the same for every citizen, otherwise it would degenerate into injustice.

ART. 7.—Every citizen being equal in rights, ought to be equally admissible to the occupation of that post which a majority of his fellow-citizens shall call upon him to hold; each citizen ought to be compelled to accept the public offices in his turn, if a majority of his fellow-citizens think fit; but no citizen ought to be obligated to hold a public situation twice, until every other citizen shall have filled the same post.

ART. 8.—Religion being a matter of opinion, ought to be free as the circumambient air. No citizen ought to be compelled to adopt any particular religious tenets, or be excluded from his rights as a citizen on account of his faith, while the manifestation of it does not tend to injure the society of which he forms a part.

ART. 9.—No citizen ought to be accused, arrested, or detained, except in cases determined by the law, and according to the forms which shall be prescribed by the law. As punishment ought to attach to illegal arrest or detention of any citizen, so no citizen ought to withhold an obedience to the law, and resistance to it becomes a crime.

ART. 10.—The law ought not to establish any punishment that is disproportioned to the crime committed; and punishment, to be legitimate, ought to have been decreed and promulgated antecedent to the offence, and be applied according to the forms prescribed.

ART. 11.—Every citizen being presumed innocent until such time as a jury of his fellow-citizens shall have declared him guilty; whenever it shall be deemed necessary to the public safety to seclude a citizen, all coercive force, not absolutely necessary to the detention of his person, ought to be criminal.

Art. 12.—The free communication of thought and of opinion is one of the most irrefragable and precious rights of a citizen. Every citizen therefore ought to be allowed freely to speak, write, and publish his sentiments and opinion, upon any and every subject, when such writing, speaking, or publishing is not injurious to the interests of individuals: the law ought, therefore, to apply remedies to the abuses of the press and of speech, only in the cases of individuals.

Art. 13.—The keeping of any armed force on foot, other than the citizens of the state, being inconsistent with the liberties of the citizens, ought to become criminal in the parties concerned: the armed force being for the benefit of all, ought not to be applied to the sole use or advantage of any individual, except in protecting his natural rights.

Art. 14.—Society has a right to reimburse those expences which it incurs, by a levy on each of its citizens; this impost ought to be equally sustained by all the citizens, according to the abilities of each.

Art. 15.—Every public functionary ought to be responsible to the society for his administration; from this responsibility he ought not to be absolved,

Art. 16.—Every citizen has the imprescriptible right by himself, or by his representative, to give his voice concerning the necessity of the contribution to be levied; it ought not to be levied without the consent of a majority of the citizens previously obtained; every individual has a right to investigate the public accounts, and any attempt to prevent the exercise of this right, is an infraction of the rights of man, and ought to attach criminality.

Art. 17.—Society ought to guarantee to every citizen the exercise of his natural and unalienable rights; whenever these are attacked, each citizen has an indefeasible right to call upon society for protection against the invader. Society ceases to be just when it refuses this assistance.

Art. 18.—Every citizen has a right to the protection of society in the enjoyment of his property honestly acquired; no power can deprive him of any part of it except when a majority of his fellow-citizens shall have declared it necessary to the safety of the state; and in that case, society is bound to make him an indemnity.

REPRESENTATION AND EXECUTIVE GOVERNMENT.

MEN, in forming themselves into societies, have tacitly made a *covenant*, by which they engage to be mutually serviceable to each other, and to do nothing that can be injurious either to their individual or collective capacity; yet the nature of man rendering it indispensibly necessary that he should at every instant search after happiness, which he always makes consist in the gratification of some passion, it becomes necessary to direct these passions in such a manner that they may concur to the general prosperity, by which alone individual happiness can be truly said to exist; for this purpose *laws* are established, by which it is or ought to be ascertained, from the united wisdom of society, what actions are or are not conducive to the maintenance of association, and the felicity of its members. But that these laws may be equitable and receive a general obedience, it is also necessary that they should at all times be the expression of the public will, indeed, whenever they are not the result of the *free consent* of a majority of the citizens who compose a state, they are an infraction of the rights of man, an unjust *usurpation,* and a direct *robbery.* And, as in numerous associations, an assembly of the whole citizens to discuss public measures is altogether impracticable, and could not be held without engendering tumults and disorder, it has been found necessary to choose from amongst the citizens individuals in whom society places a confidence, to be the organs by which the general will, that is to say, the will of the majority of the citizens, is expressed ; these are intrusted with a certain degree of power, to make such regulations and laws as they may judge expedient and necessary to the happiness and well-being of the community of which they themselves form a part.

CORRUPTION, that dreadful weapon in the hands of wicked and designing men, found means to spread its baneful influence into this wholesome and salutary institution, and by degrees to enlarge the powers of the deputy by restricting those of the elector: till at length the most profligate of the representatives, in many instances, separated themselves from their companions; assumed the sovereign authority, and having surreptitiously obtained the command of the public force, they turned that which was originally meant for the protection of society, against society itself; and through the ignorance and stupidity of man, thus made the abject slave of those who first received their appointments from him, the servant became the master: use familiarized them to the assumption; ignorance and credulity concurred to rivet their shackles; until, at last, man entirely lost sight of the first intention of his association, and in his delirium and blindness, he committed for these very men who had usurped over him an absolute authority, the most cruel and oppressive acts against his fellow-citizens; the interests of society were divided, and man became an easy prey to the ambitious and designing knave.

Elevated souls at different periods, feeling the natural dignity of man debased, his rights torn from him, and commiserating the wretchedness which every where pervades human association, have endeavoured to draw society out of this state of degradation, and place its members once more in the possession of their legislative rights; but an unfortunate principle that has hitherto infused itself into almost all their schemes, I mean that of dividing the representative and executive power, and making certain situations hereditary, has rendered, for the greater part, their most strenuous efforts nugatory and abortive.

And as the sending men to legislate without giving them the necessary power to carry their laws into execution would be an absurdity; so the separation of the executive and representative body, seems to have had its origin in an intention to deceive and defraud the people of their just rights; under a pretext as flimsy as it is fallacious; and not from any evident demonstration of its being productive of superior benefits to society: therefore, I propose that the representative and executive government shall be the same. The great desideratum then seems to be, to obtain a perfect and practicable equality of representation; and to give to every citizen a due participation in the choice of those persons to whom is delegated the power of disposing of a part of that property, which can only legitimately be the offspring of industry, and of making those laws which may abridge a part of man's original liberty, in order to secure the safety and felicity of every component member of the Commonwealth; and here I must dissent from that distinction, which has hitherto been held as an axiom not to be departed

from, that of causing property, and not persons, to be re-
presented; and my reason for thus dissenting is this, that in
all cases it is persons, and not property, that must protect
both the laws and society; for all the gold, silver, and other
valuables that ever came out of the bowels of the earth, could
never have been able, without the assistance of men's bodies,
to have protected a single individual against the depredations
of rapacious villains and titled robbers. Property, therefore, in my opinion, should never be considered in any other
light than as an adventitious circumstance, enabling the citizen who possesses it to gratify more sensual appetites than
the citizen who has no such appendage; but as by no means
giving the possessor any advantage in point of right or privilege over his poorer fellow-citizen, whose body, without
this casualty, will form as strong a rampart against the
enemies of society, as that of the richest nabob that ever
left the insulted and enslaved shores of Hindostan, glutted
with *blood, diamonds,* and *wretchedness!*

I therefore propose that the COMMONWEALTH, shall be
divided into districts, containing, as nearly as possible, each
twenty-five thousand inhabitants intitled to vote; that is to
say, male citizens, who shall have attained the age of
eighteen years, and who shall not be incapacited by crime
or insanity; and that this may be obtained as precisely as
possible, I propose that a general census of the people should
be taken, and when the districts are formed, the inhabitants
of each shall choose, from amongst themselves, by an absolute majority, that is to say, by not less than *twelve thousand five hundred and one* suffrages, a fit and proper
person to be their *register,* or keeper of the archives; whose
functions shall consist in enroling the names of all the inhabitants of the district qualified to vote; which qualification,
as I have before stated, shall only be, *having attained
eighteen years, being a male undltainted by crime, of sane
intellect, and a native of the country, or if not native, one
who shall have passed in his favour, by an absolute majority of the whole representative body, a vote of* denization.

This *registry* ought to be at all times open to the inspection
of the citizens of the district to which it shall belong, and
no one ought to have the right of citizenship who shall have
neglected to enter his name, situation, and place of abode in
the Register: and he shall, at the time of enrolment, be
obliged to bring *two citizens,* whose names shall already be
on the register, as vouchers to prove his qualification and
right to be so enregistered, and any citizen who shall give a

false voucher for another in order to obtain his enrolment,
shall, upon such falsity being proved to the satisfaction of a
jury, be disenfranchised for seven years; and, if convicted
of a second offence, for ever; but this in no case to affect his
children; and in order that the citizen who may happen to
have residences in different districts, shall not be, from that
circumstance, enabled to obtain an undue influence over his
fellow-citizens, by having in consequence a plurality of votes,
I propose that the citizen being possessed of such different
abodes, shall, at the time of his being enregistered, give in
the titles and designations of such habitations, in each district
where such possessions may be, signifying in each the district in which he means to exercise his right of suffrage,
and this, under penalty of forfeiture for seven years of his
elective franchise for the first offence, and perpetually for
the second, upon conviction before a jury of having given
in a false account to the register: the same regulations to
be observed upon any citizen becoming possessed of any
other residence subsequent to his enrolment; the account
to be given in ten days next after such acquisition, provided
no election shall intervene during the ten days; should that
happen, he shall then be bound to do it immediately; and in
case of removal from one district to another, he shall ob-
serve the same mode of procedure, giving notice to the
register to strike off his name from the roll of the district
from which he shall depart. And I propose that every fourth
day a list of all cases of death, crimination, and lunacy,
shall be published by the municipal officers, and be by them
transmitted to the register of the district, that he may accordingly rectify his registry. And, that no district may
increase or diminish in too great a degree, and thereby render
the representation unequal,—I propose, that every *third*
year the representative body shall have laid before them the
different registers, that they may compare the numbers of
each, and join together, or separate, or otherwise modify
such as shall have increased or decreased in such manner,
that each body of electors may be composed as nearly as
possible of *twenty-five thousand* citizens possessing the
elective franchise, who shall be entitled to send *four* representatives. And, as I propose that in the Commonwealth
no place or office of any kind shall be held for a longer time
than *one year,* so I propose, that one month previous to
the exp'ration of each year, the citizens shall, by a number
of twelve thousand five hundred and one electors, being an
absolute majority of each district, choose a register for the

year ensuing: the *salary* of the *register* to be fixed at *three bushels of wheat per diem*, or a consideration 'in' money equal to the value of such wheat, to be ascertained' by 'the respective returns of the average price of grain in the district where he is chosen. His *qualifications* to be being *a resident in the district, and having elective franchise, having attained the age of twenty-five years, uncontaminated by crime, and of a sane mind.* The mode of *election* to be by *ballot.*

· The manner of electing the *four representatives* for each district of twenty-five thousand electors, I propose to be by ballot, to take place one month previous to the expiration of each year; the only period for which I propose they should enjoy their representative capacity; no citizen to be declared to have been chosen unless he has an absolute majority of the citizens having elective franchise in his favour; that is to say, not having a less number of votes than *twelve thousand five hundred and one.* ·

The qualification for a representative to be, having attained the age of twenty-five years, having been an inhabitant of the district which he is to represent for the year antecedent to his election, having elective franchise, that is to say, being uncontaminated by crime, and of a sane mind.

The representative to be incapable of holding any other public situation or office during the year of his deputation; and to be paid *four bushels* of wheat per diem, or an equivalent in money equal to the wheat, taking the average price of the grain in the district where the representative body meet, for the standard: and to be allowed such travelling expences as a jury of *twenty-five* of his constituents shall deem reasonable; the jury for this purpose to be chosen by lot.

At the same time, when the election for the four representatives takes place, I also propose that there shall be chosen four *supernumeraries,* who shall succeed 'to 'the representation in case of the death of the member, or of his impeachment, or removal, &c. and to perform the duty of the representative in case of sickness; the supernumerary to receive the same salary as the representative when on actual service; and to be allowed travelling expences, to be settled by jury as already stated; and in case of his succeeding to the representation by the death or dismissal of the former member, then the citizens of the district to proceed immediately to choose another supernumerary.

I also propose, that the electors shall, at any time when

they shall (to the number of *twelve thousand five hundred and one*,) agree that the representative or his supernumerary has forfeited their confidence, be possessed of the power of removing such deputy or his supernumerary, and proceed to the election of another.

COMMITTEE OF GOVERNMENT.

The representative body, when met, shall proceed to choose from amongst their own bod , a *Committee of Government*, to be elected by ballot, and each member to be considered only as having his election by having in his favour an actual majority of the representative body: for example, if the deputies consist of four hundred citizens, then it shall be absolutely necessary for each member chosen into the committee of government, to have the suffrages of *two hundred and one* representatives. I also propose, that four of the members of the committee shall go out monthly by rotation, and be replaced by four others chosen in the same manner as the first. This committee to have no other power than that of executing the decrees of the representation, and laying before them, for consideration, such measures as they may deem necessary to the public advantage ; but not to put any measure into execution until after it shall have received the sanction of an absolute majority of the representatives of the people. This committee to have under them *six clerks*, to be chosen anually from among the people, by an absolute majority of the representative body, one month previous to the expiration of each year ; each to be paid *two bushels* of wheat per diem, or an equivalent in money at the average price of grain in the district where the representatives shall hold their sittings.

COMMITTEE OF FINANCE.

I also propose, that the representative body shall choose from amongst themselves, observing the same forms as in the choice of the members composing the Committee of Government, a *Committee of Finance*, to consist of twelve members *four* of which shall go out monthly by rotation, and be replaced in the same manner as the citizens of the committee of government. This committee to have under them *six clerks*, to be chosen from amongst the people, in the same manner as the clerks of the Committee of Government ; and each to be paid *two bushels* of wheat per diem, or an equivalent in money according to the value of the wheat at the average market price of such district where the representative body are assembled.

The functions of this committee, I propose, to be the receipt of the taxes; the care of the national treasure; and the payment of all salaries: the inspection of public roads, buildings, canals, and rivers, and to report to the representative body, when and where it is necessary to amend old ones, or make new ones ; but not to put them into execution until they shall have been decreed by an absolute majority of the national representation. It shall be their duty to inspect the public works of every sort, and make the necessary payments; but, previous to any such payment taking place, they shall report upon it to the representative body, and receive their sanction. Their accounts to be always subject to the inspection of the citizens composing the representation, and every month they shall publish an account of their receipts and expenditures, and of the money in their hands, signed by the names of the whole committee, with the names of the districts they represent; these accounts shall be deposited with the registers of each district for the inspection of the citizens.

COMMITTEE OF AGRICULTURE, TRADE, AND PROVISIONS.

I also propose, that the representative body shall choose from among themselves, a *committee of agriculture, trade, and provisions*, observing the same forms as in the two other committees, four of which shall vacate their stations monthly, by rotation, and be replaced in the same manner as in the other committees. This committee to have under them *six clerks*, chosen from among the citizens in the same manner as the clerks to the other committees, and each to be paid *two bushels* of wheat per diem, or an equivalent in money, at the average price of the district where the representation are communed.

The functions of this committee, I propose, to be the inspection of the agriculture of the country ; the state of the trade ; and the taking measures for providing provisions and fuel for the different districts ; they shall every month make a report to the national representation, signed by all the members composing the committee, stating the districts which they represent ; these reports, I propose, shall be sent to the registers of each district for public information.

The qualification for a *clerk* to the *committees* to be, having attained the age of twenty-one years, and having elective

4

franchise, that is to say, uncontaminated with crime, of sane intellect, a native of the country, or naturalized.

I also propose, to prevent any stagnation taking place in the prosecution of the public business, that at the dissolution of one representative body, the *committees* who shall be in office, shall remain until they are replaced by the regular monthly succession of four members of the new representation.

And as laws, to be equitable, should always be the expression of the will of the majority of the citizens, I propose, that no act, regulation, or decree, shall take place and have effect, or be binding on the citizens, unless it has received the sanction of an absolute majority of the whole representation; that is to say, if the deputies are five hundred in number, then to every act that shall have force, two hundred and fifty-one members shall have given their assent; and their names, and those of the districts which they represent, shall be annexed to every such decree on its promulgation; or else it shall be considered as void, and of no effect. Thus every act of the *legislature* being sanctioned by an absolute majority of the *deputies*, and these representatives being themselves deputed by an actual majority of the citizens, it would be a fair inference to suppose all such acts to be the expression of the public will, and to convey, as nearly as human possibility admits, the genuine sense of the community. The same inference will hold good with respect to the Committee of Executive Government, which, being chosen by an absolute majority of the representative body, to which every citizen is eligible, whatever they do may be justly considered as springing from the free consent of a majority of the whole citizens. I propose also, that a copy of every act of the *legislature* be sent, properly signed, to the registers of each district, for public inspection, and also to the offices of the *judicial administrators*.

But as the long possession of power has been found, by experience, to corrupt the human mind, and make men take illegal and surreptitious means to continue the enjoyment of it, I propose, to remedy this evil, hitherto found to be fraught with such destructive consequences to the liberty of the human species, that after having served the office of representative for one year, the citizen shall be incapable of being again chosen for two years after; this will have two good effects—the one will be, that the representative, being necessitated to return into the mass of the citizens, will be

careful not to give his sanction to any arbitrary measure, because he will, in that case, be subjected himself, for two
years, to all the evils of his own decrees ;—the other is, that
by this means, the business of legislating and governing
will be more generally diffused amongst the people ; and thus
the principle of public happiness will become more universally understood, and the opportunities of *corruption* be considerably if not entirely removed.

ADMINISTRATION OF THE ·LAWS.

As I 'conceive that. the administration of laws, which
ought to be made only with a view to the public good, requires
nothing more than integrity and industry ; and, as nothing
can be more unjust, or implicate a greater absurdity, than
that those institutions, which are meant for the benefit of all,
should be exercised for the particular profit and advantage of
a few ;' so the establishment of attorneys, counsel, judges,
&c. to be paid by the individual who feels it necessary to
recur to the justice of his country, seems to be a practice
that has originated in corruption, the continuation of which
must ultimately be destructive of all morality, and subversive
of that equality of judicial administration, that alone can
render it beneficial and estimable in the eyes of men. It
is the boast, indeed, of some countries, that the law is equally
open to the rich and the poor; the same may be said of a
banker's shop ; but as it needs no argument to prove, that
in the latter instance, the man who is unprovided with a
good draft will not be allowed to receive money: so it is
equally demonstrable, that, in those countries where the
law is administered at private expence, the man who is destitute of a long purse, will be equally unable to obtain either
law or justice. Thus, in such countries, the rich man is
enabled to lord it over his poorer neighbour with impunity.
This generates strife amongst the citizens, and divides their
interests, which, that they may retain their liberty, and live
in perfect security, they should always endeavour to con-
centrate and unite.

I propose, therefore, that in each district the citizens shall
choose, annually, from amongst their own body, by an absolute majority, a citizen, whose duty it shall be to preside
over all complaints, both criminal and civil, that may arise
in the district, and adjudge them, with the assistance of a
jury, to be chosen by lot from the registry of the district,
according to the laws of the Commonweath. This *judicial*

administrator, I propose, to be assisted by *three clerks*, who shall also be chosen by an absolute majority of the electors of the district yearly: the election to take place one month previously to the expiration of each year. This tribunal, I propose, shall be open every day for the distribution of justice. To all parties accused, I propose giving the right of a peremptory challenge to as many jurymen as the number of which the jury by which they are to be tried shall be composed. Thus suppose *fifteen* citizens to be a jury, and this is the number I would propose; *thirty* shall be summoned by lot, out of which he shall have a right to reject fifteen: the other *fifteen* to try the cause, with the assistance of the administrator of justice, who shall read the law upon the case, and in the event of the party accused being found guilty, pass the sentence affixed by the law immediately, and in all those cases, where the punishment is not precisely expressed by the legislature of the Commonwealth, then the jury to award such punishment as they shall deem consistent with equity; and if the party sentenced under this last circumstance be dissatisfied, then an appeal to lie to the Committee of Executive Government, who shall report the affair to the representation, an absolute majority of which shall finally decide the cause.

I also propose, that the same jury shall never try two successive causes, either criminal or civil; but that for as many causes as there are to be tried, so many times thirty jurymen shall be chosen by lot, and summoned to attend; the names to be enrolled, and called over in rotation, and each *fifteen*, as they are left after the challenges, to be the jury to try the cause. This will prevent the possibility of bribing a jury, because it will be utterly impossible to know what jury will try any given cause.

The qualification for a judicial administrator to be, having attained his thirtieth year, having been a resident in the district for three years previous to his election, having the elective franchise, that is to say uncontaminated with crime, and of sane mind.—His remuneration to be fixed at *three bushels* of wheat per diem, or an equivalent in money, at the average market price of the district.

The qualification of a clerk to be, having attained twenty-five years, having resided in the district for two years antecedent to his election, and having elective franchise: the salary to be *two bushels* of wheat per diem, or an equivalent in money.

I also propose, that the laws should be administered immediately, and without intermission, allowing only to the
parties the time necessary to prepare their documents; and
in no case do I propose that the administration of justice
shall be attended with one farthing expence to either party,
except what a jury shall adjudge against those parties whose
suits they may pronounce litigious and vexatious; for as
justice ought to be distributive and impartially administered,
nothing can be more absurd than to make the obtaining of
it a matter of expence to the citizen who applies for it; this
being, in fact, nothing more than establishing a dangerous
pre-eminence in the man of property over his more needy
neighbour, and deciding the point in dispute by the strength
of the purse, and completely and effectually secluding
poverty, from obtaining that redress which is equally its
right with the greatest *wealth* and *affluence*.

LIBERTY OF THE PRESS.

This being one of the most sacred rights of a citizen, and
perhaps the only means of ascertaining, what most certainly
ought to be the principal object of every citizen's pursuit,
truth, I propose, that in the Commonwealth, in no possible
case shall any restriction be laid on the writing, publishing,
or delivering any discourse or opinion, on any subject whatever. Indeed, *truth* being the end most desirable in all well
regulated states, the investigation of principles ought to be
free to every one, and rather meet with encouragement than
restraint; therefore no licence or authority ought to be necessary for the printing, publishing, or delivery of any doctrine, or of any animadversion on the public administration;
and these are my reasons; the doctrine, if good, and capable
of producing a majority of the people to declare in its favour,
ought, most assuredly, to be received; if otherwise, its own
want of importance will be its surest and best destruction
with freemen; and all experience has shewn, that the attempt to suppress opinions is the most infallible means of
bringing them into esteem: indeed, that which in itself is
stupid and irrational, does not want the keen and critical eye
of a public accuser to point out its absurdity; and if it is
reasonable and just, it only marks the ignorance, folly, and
wickedness, of those who are willing to smother it; for in a
Commonwealth, where every one has an equal interest in
supporting the happiness and tranquillity of the nation, no
one will be able, by any argument, however plausible, to

injure a society whose members will, at all times, be ready
to resist every attempt at subverting that felicity of which
they feel the beneficent effect. Thus, when the government shall be *rational, just*, and *equitable*, all the citizens
will find their greatest advantage in defending it from insi-
dious attacks, and they will be a much better security for
its stability than *prosecutions for high treason, or imprison-
ments for sedition*. The wings of *liberty* are deprived of
their feathers whenever the Press is laid under restraint,

In cases of *libel* on private characters, I propose, that
the person who makes the attack, if called upon, shall either
be bound to substantiate the charge, or be liable to such
penalty as a *jury of fifteen men*, chosen by lot, shall inflict,
and also the citizen convicted, shall be deprived, *for seven
years*, of his elective franchise.

INHERITANCE AND BASTARDY.

I propose that, in all cases, the children shall divide, in
equal portions, the property of which the father may die
possessed; if the wife be also alive, she shall be entitled to
participate, and receive her dividend accordingly: when she
dies, I propose, the children shall again divide equally.

. And as nothing can possibly exceed the cruelty and injustice of the laws of bastardy, which are, in fact, *inflicting
punishment on those who never yet had it in their power
to offend*, I propose, that in the division of the father's effects,
all the children, without exception, shall be included, whether
born in wedlock or otherwise, for if any crime can attach, it
must be to the father and mother, and not to the child, who
is brought into this world without his consent; and surely
no one will attempt to deny that the bastard, as he is called
by the crooked policy of some governments, is as much the
child of the father, and a citizen of the state, as the present
legitimate inheritors of the parents' wealth. These laws,
which seem to have originated in an intention to restrain
men from forming promiscuous connexions, like most others,
have been found, by experience, to be sadly deficient in
means to the end proposed. Indeed, what absurdity can be
more apparent than making those the only sufferers by any
particular act, who had no knowledge or share in the com-
mission of it. Would it not be considered as iniquitous, to
hang the son because the father had committed a robbery?—
And yet the laws of bastardy form a parallel case in all those
countries where they have existence. In my apprehension,

the only result of the laws of bastardy, is the rendering a certain portion of the citizens vicious and the enemies of those societies who deprive them in the most cruel and unjust manner of the immunities of a citizen, for that in which they participated not, and could not avoid.

In cases where there are no children to inherit, I propose, the possessor of property to be at liberty to leave it as he pleases; and if he dies intestate, the property to go to his nearest relation.

PRICE OF LABOUR.

And that the *industrious manufacturer, labourer,* or *cultivator,* may at all times be enabled to live comfortably, and bring up his family in a manner suitable to become good and useful citizens, and that they may never be oppressed, by their richer associates, I propose, that no labourer or workman shall be paid at a less rate for his day's labour than *one bushel* of wheat, or the value of it in money, at the average market price of the district were he is employed.— This will always enable him to satisfy all the real wants of his nature, and make provision for his old age; and surely no one can be more justly entitled to be rendered comfortable than he who by his labour contributes to the comfort and happiness of others. I also propose, that every citizen shall be at liberty to follow that occupation which most pleases him, and in any part of the Commonwealth without restriction.

REGISTER OF BIRTHS AND BURIALS.

I propose, that all citizens shall, on pain of losing their rights of citizenship, be obliged to give in regularly an account of all *births* and *deaths* that take place in their families to the municipal officers, who shall transmit them. every fourth day; to the register of the district. I also propose, that no dead body shall be suffered to be interred at a less distance than *one furlong* from the city, village, or town, because experience has proved, that suffering burial grounds in populous places is destructive of health.

PUBLIC TAXES.

When taxes are levied on the people, they ought to be of such description that they fall as equally as possible on all the citizens, according to their respective abilities; and not to be of such a nature as to be easily avoided, because, this again has a tendency to separate the interests of the citizens, which all institutions ought to endeavour to unite; for this purpose the only tax I would propose in the Commonwealth, is so much per acre on land, to be paid yearly, by the citizens, when they go to ballot for representatives, into the hands of the *register;* any citizen who shall neglect to pay his quota, or use any kind of subterfuge to avoid paying for his full number of acres, to forfeit four times the tax. The *committee of agriculture, trade, and provisions,* shall cause surveys to be made in the different districts; and each citizen, when he enrolls his name with the register, to declare the number of acres he holds absolutely in his own possession; but as the tax thus levied would be extremely small, it would scarcely be a temptation for any one to evade it; and in this mode it would be collected without expence. I calculate that *fourpence* per acre would overpay all the expences of a *good* government. These taxes to be pa d into the hands of the *committee of finance,* and to be deposited in the national treasury, within one month after the receipt. This would preclude those hordes of *tax-gathere s, excisemen,* and *custom-house officers,* that swarm in every country and are almost always the enemies of the people.

RELIGION.

I propose, that this being entirely a matter of opinion, in which no one can prove his infallibility, the Commonwealth should not adopt any particular religious tenet, nor pay any priest, of any persuasion, nor build any house of religious worship ; but that each citizen should be left entirely at his liberty to follow that form of religion which is most accordant to his ideas. On no account would I propose that it should interfere in any manner with the political government of the Commonwealth nor ever allow it to become a subject of discussion in the *legislature.*

BREAD AND FUEL.

These being articles of the first necessity, without which human nature cannot long subsist, the supply of them to the citizens at an easy rate should of consequence form a prominent feature in the administration of every good government; for nothing can be more scandalous, or a greater reproach to any government in any country, than either to see a scarcity of these necessary articles, or that they should be at an exorbitant price, I therefore propose, that the

Committee of Agriculture, Trade, and Provisions, shall make it an indispensible part of their duty to see that every district has a proper supply of these commodities at 'the most reasonable rates; and in those places that depend for a supply from other parts of the Commonwealth by water carriage, I propose, that they shall establish large national magazines, in which six months' provision of these necessaries shall always be kept ready for the public use: this will prevent the prices being affected by frost, or other casualties, and enable the inhabitants to be continually in the enjoyment of a plentiful supply at a moderate price. And that this object may be continually kept in view, I propose, that the registers shall make a monthly report of their districts, on this subject, to the *Committee of Agriculture, Trade, and Provisions*, who shall lay them regularly before the national representation, with their own remarks. The registers and the committees to be answerable for the truth of their statements. This mode would destroy those disgraceful monopolies that frequently render these articles so dear as scarcely to be within the reach of the poor. In England, if this mode was pursued, *coals* would never exceed *six-pence* or *seven-pence* the bushel; or *bread three-pence*, or *four-pence* the quartern loaf, even under the present system.

MARRIAGE.

It is, I believe, an incontrovertible principle, that the strength of a state depends upon the number of its citizens; to encourage population, therefore, should be the maxim of all wise governments; for this purpose they tell us, the marriage-ceremony in most countries was instituted; but I apprehend it will not be denied, that to render this means adequate to its end, it should necessarily be productive of the felicity of the parties contracting: this can never be the case while two persons, who, after living together for a certain time, find their tempers unaccordant, and whose manners are but little calculated to promote each other's happiness, have no power to dissolve the bond of their union, from henceforth, contrary to nature, and useless to the purpose for which it was designed, that of procreating their species, and augmenting human happiness. The hymeneal lamp expires when love ceases to furnish oil To remedy this evil, and render the connubial state really conducive to the happiness and increase of the human species, I propose, that *marriage* shall be merely a civil

5

contract, and be entered into before the magistrate of the place, unattended with expence, a copy of it being transmitted to the register of the district; and that it shall at all times be liable to dissolution, upon sufficient cause being shewn to a jury, who shall be immediately summoned, upon the complaint of either the husband or wife, to the administrator of the district.   This would prevent those shameful bickerings that but too frequently send the husband one way and the wife another, to their mutual destruction; because any thing is preferable to the company of those who have ceased to merit our affections.   I also propose, that the male, at the age of eighteen, and the female, at the age of sixteen, shall be deemed marriageable.   This will have a tendency to lessen those dreadful scenes of wretched pollution that every where disgrace the moral institutions of civilized nations, and which are principally kept in existence by the impolitic restraints which have been laid on the youth of both sexes entering into the hymeneal bonds at a period when nature has given vigour to their passions, and that greediness of wealth that frequently induces parents to oblige their children to render themselves unhappy for life, by an intermarriage with decrepitude, age, or a person that is their utter aversion, merely because it is what the world very unjustly calls *a prudent match.*   Thus the youth, disgusted at home, seeks amongst those unfortunate females, whom a similar policy has driven into a state of prostitution, to satisfy those passions that nature has implanted strongly in his breast.   I therefore propose, that no consent whatever shall be necessary to the junction of a male and female, except their own; for as this is a matter in which their future happiness or misery is concerned, it seems but rational and just that they alone should be consulted on an affair of such importance to their welfare.   These regulations would also remedy another evil, which is the immense expence that attends the obtaining of a divorce in most countries, and which frequently obliges a man and a woman, for want of the money necessary, to live together, although they are conscious of each other's infidelity.

CANALS, PUBLIC ROADS, AND RIVERS.

I also propose, that no canal shall be dug, public road made, or river cleansed, at other than public expence; and this is my reason,—these things being a benefit to the whole community, either immediately or consequently, ought to be defrayed by the generality of the citizens; they will also, by this means, be done much better and more effectually. I propose, therefore, that when the inhabitants of any place, shall deem it necessary to widen a river, make a road, or cut a canal, they shall lay, their observations ·before the · *Committee of Finance,* who shall cause inspection to be made, and report thereon to the representative body immediately, on pain of impeachment for neglect. In every well-regulated state, *canals* should intersect the whole country, in order to facilitate the transport of the superfluity of one part to another, at easy rates, and diminish the breed · of horses, who consume that produce which ought to nourish man, and by this means increase the price of provisions.

WASTE LANDS.

The existence of these are a reproach to any government, because they have a tendency to check population, and augment the price of provisions, both of which are in their consequences injurious to the Commonwealth, however beneficial they may be to some few of its members. I therefore propose, that no land whatever shall be suffered to remain uncultivated, either for parks, pleasure-grounds, common, or, otherwise; but that the *Committee of Agriculture, Trade, and Provisions,* shall make it their duty continually to see that all the soil of the Commonwealth is in a state of culture, either for pasturage or produce ; and in case of any citizen's refusing to cultivate any part of his lands, the Committee · shall take such lands into their own hands, and cause them to be cultivated for the benefit of the state, reserving half the profits towards defraying the public expenditure, and · paying the other half into the hands of the owner of the land, who shall 'be permitted to reclaim them, on giving six citizens, having elective franchise, as security for their future cultivation. To see an acre of land uncultivated, and a citizen without employ in the same state, denotes a culpable inattention in the legislature, and demands the strictest enquiry of the citizens into the causes of this, shameful neglect.

MAGISTRACY.

Every *town, city,* and *large village,* I propose, should have a *municipal officer,* with clerks to assist him, for the regulation of the police ; these officers and clerks, I propose, to be chosen yearly, by ballot, by an actual majority of the whole inhabitants of the municipality, having elective franchise ; the number of these municipalities to be settled by the national representation, marking the dependencies of each. The salaries of these municipal officers to be *three bushels* of wheat per diem ; their clerks *two bushels* of wheat per diem ; to be paid by the inhabitants of the municipality, and to be assessed yearly by a jury of *twenty-five* of the citizens of the municipality, to be chosen by lot.

LAME, BLIND, LUNATICS, DEAF, AND DUMB.

These descriptions of citizens being in most instances incapacitated by nature from contributing by their exertions to the common stock, most justly claim the support of their more favoured fellow-citizens; I therefore propose, that all such, after declaration of the fact by a jury of *twenty-five* men of the district, chosen by lot, shall be pensioners of the Commonwealth, and receive *one bushel* of wheat per diem, or its equivalent in money, unless the jury are of opinion that their circumstances do not require it. For such *lunatics,* whose being at liberty may be deemed prejudicial to society, by a jury of *twenty-five*, chosen by lot, public edifices should be erected ; these to be under inspection of the *committee* of *forty ;* the *keeper* to be chosen yearly by an absolute majority of the representative body.

PUBLIC PRISONS.

If such disgraceful buildings, which are always a reproach to the legislative body, and can scarcely ever obtain in a well-regulated state of society, are rendered necessary by the degeneracy and corruption of man, at least they ought to be rendered the instruments of public utility, and the means of re-conducting the citizens into the paths of *truth, virtue,* and *reason ;* and not as they are in most countries, the nurseries of vice and infamy, where the novice is hardened in crime, and the profligate loses all sense of shame and of their duty to their country.

I therefore propose, that in those districts where the national representation shall deem it expedient to have prisons, they shall always be situated at least two miles from any city or town, in an open airy situation ; that the *keeper* and his servants shall be chosen yearly, by an absolute majority of the citizens of the district, having elective franchise, that is to say, by the suffrage of *twelve thousand five hundred and one* votes ; that they shall be paid by the nation, and not suffered on any account to take any fee or other emolument whatever from the unhappy citizens committed to their care, on pain of attaching criminality; their salaries to be *three bushels* of wheat per diem to the keeper, and *two bushels* to each of his servants, or an equivalent in money. And that no extortion or other ill treatment of prisoners may obtain, I propose, that *three* members of the legislative body shall be chosen by an absolute majority of the representation, every month, who shall visit all the prisons, and make a report, signed with their names and the districts they represent, to the representation; this report shall be printed and sent regularly to the register of the districts for public inspection. I also propose, that all the prisoners shall be made to work at some useful occupation ; the profits of their labour to be their own property, after deducting a certain portion towards defraying the expence of the prison establishment, unless otherwise decreed by their jury, and during their seclusion to be fed at the charge of the Commonwealth, in a mode to be settled by the representation.

ABOLITION OF CAPITAL PUNISHMENTS.

As nothing can be more unnatural than that man should destroy his fellow-man, so society, in my opinion, can never acquire the right of inflicting the punishment of death on any of its citizens ; indeed, even in cases of murder, the deprivation of the life of the murderer is only redoubling the loss already sustained by the Commonwealth. I should therefore propose the abolition of all capital punishments, and in their place substituting some mode of making those whose offences may be deemed of a capital nature, work hard the remainder of their lives, for the benefit of the community they have injured; for society commits *suicide* every time it deprives itself of the services of any of its members, merely because they have already injured it.

EDUCATION.

I have now reached what I conceive to be the most interesting and important of all human objects, since from it springs the only permanent liberty and durable happiness of man,—*the culture of the human mind and the education of the members who compose society,*—and this should of course form an institution that ought to be considered of the first consequence to the Commonwealth, and be cordially cherished by all the citizens.

There needs no argument to prove the pains that have been taken by despots, priests, and usurpers, to keep the bulk of the people in a state of the most savage ignorance;

almost every page of history, as well ancient as modern, is a
strong and irrefragable evidence of their malign and wicked
endeavours. They well knew the importance of education ;
they were not unacquainted that *knowledge* and *liberty* went
hand in hand, and that wherever the first prevailed generally,
the latter must be the inevitable consequence; they were
perfectly aware that an enlightened people would not consent to that shameful degradation of their species, of becoming the vile slaves and abettors of *lawless oppressors, sanguinary tyrants,* and *peculating adventurers ;* they felt
that man, cultivated and educated, would consider his fellow-
man only as a man, and not as a god, or being of a superior
order. To prevent, therefore, this salutary institution from
obtaining (which would immediately tend to a total subver-
sion of their usurped power) formed the most prominent and
most interesting speculation of every chief. But it was to be
done with art and circumspection, with the apparent consent
of the citizens, and not by prohibitory laws, which would
at once have blown up this *mine of infamy,* and have
opened the eyes of those whom it was necessary, to further
their own views, and that they might be enabled to continue
with impunity their nefarious practices, to keep in a state of
utter blindness. To effectuate this iniquitous scheme, and
to prevent education from sending froth its irradiating beams
amongst the citizens, required Machiavelian skill, and more
than common duplicity and adroitness ; because it was indispensibly requisite, for this purpose, to have the appearance
of encouraging that which they meant most effectually to
smother and destroy ; we therefore see the greatest despots
encouraging men of letters at their courts, and founding
universities, but we at the same time have the melancholy
spectacle of their fixing the price of labour at so low a rate
as completely secludes the laborious citizen, who lives by
his industry alone, from any hope of being able to maintain
the expence of educating his children ;- we see them lay
heavy imposts on all the necessaries of life, thus rendering it
absolutely requisite to employ that time which ought to be
dedicated to education, in hard labour to support existence ;
we see them, under every kind of specious pretext, clogging
with stamps and other duties the free circulation of knowledge ; we see newspapers put under inquisitorial laws,
and in most countries we see licencers of publications established, who are careful in rejecting all those works that
have any tendency to conduct to the people to *truth* and
reason, and make them throw off the bandeau of *supersti-*

tion, falsehood, and *tyranny:* the theatres are shackled in the same manner. By these practices, education and the means of acquiring information has been confined to a small circle of citizens, who have always been either bought over by the friends of a rapacious government, or hunted down by oppression, if they have ever presumed the attempting to illuminate the mind, and enlighten the understanding of the mass of mankind ; unintelligible and technical terms have been introduced into all the sciences, and thus by a combination of circumstances that have had all the shew of accident and casualty, although in fact they are connected links of the great and heavy chain, that has been villainously forged to bind man down in the most degrading ignorance; knowledge and instruction has been ingrossed by the few, to the injury of the many, and has been made a lucrative trade in the hands of those, who, seduced by corrupt influence, have, instead of imparting it generally, most scandalously abused it, from a conviction that they were in no fear of detection by the generality of their fellow-citizens, and concurred in the great but diabolical plan of maintaining *ignorance, credulity,* and *superstition,* by means of which men have been made *slaves.* Indeed, education has been so very rare and uncommon, that those who have possessed this advantage, have generally obtained a great degree of credit with the people ; who, though not permitted themselves to experience its beneficent effects, have always admired it in others. *Corruption* saw this with pleasure, besieged and subdued the greater part of the learned ; *oppression* and *tyranny* putting flight those few honest men who opposed its attacks, thus turning to advantage this disposition in the people, which they seemed to gratify. These venal sons of education thus gained over, readily lent their aid to perpetuate abuses in which they were now become interested, to rivet closely the fetters of a tyranny in which they were permitted to participate, and keep man in a state of abject slavery, by rooting in him ignorance and folly, to prevent their own iniquitous measures from being discovered ; nay, some of these have even so infamously disgraced themselves, and been such vile tools in the hands of corruption, as to write treatises to prove that man's felicity was considerably diminished and abridged by literary acquirements, and that the more ignorant the man, the more completely happy his condition. In consequence, falsehood has every where obtained; systems of error have been established, and men have been left to grope in blindness their way through those dark caverns, into which the cunning of priests and tyrants have precipitated them ; and which their infernal policy has always prevented from being enlightened by the sacred and brilliant rays of *education, knowledge*, and *truth*, which alone can conduct them to the groves of happiness.

To restore then liberty to long-insulted man, to draw immortal and immutable *truth* out of those 'holes and corners into which falsehood, superstition, and tyranny has driven it, and place it on those altars which are at present occupied by *error*, and to remove that disgraceful ignorance, which debases human nature, rendering it corrupt, venal, and profligate, I intend that *education* shall form a part of the national establishment of the Commonwealth, and be considered as one of the first objects of the legislator's care, because to form good and virtuous citizens for a state, it is absolutely necessary that they should be instructed in their rights, know how to maintain them, and be acquainted with their nature and consequence. I therefore propose, that in each district there shall be erected a sufficient number of *public schools*, to educate all the children of the district, and that from the age of four to fourteen, no citizen shall be suffered to withhold his child from receiving an education at one of the public seminaries of the district in which he resides, upon pain of forfeiting his rights as a citizen for ever ; and that the rising generation may at all times receive the impulse of the public will, and that each parent may have a due share in and controul over the education of his child, I propose, that every year the *masters, mistresses*, or *tutors*, shall be elected by ballot, by an absolute majority of the electors of the district, that is to say, by the suffrage of not less than *twelve thousand five hundred and one ;* the new election to take place one month previous to the expiration of each year ; and each master, mistress, or tutor, to receive a salary of *four bushels* of wheat per diem, or an equivalent in money, taking the average market price of the district, and to live rent free in the national school, which shall always be the property of the Commonwealth, and be fitted up with a library, and with mathematical, astronomical, optical, and other scientific apparatus, for the use of the pupils ; the children to be clothed, boarded, and lodged during the ten years of their education, at the public expence, and without any distinction whatever ; the expence to be borne by the inhabitants of the district by assessment.

And to prevent abuses taking place in these establishments, and to ensure a punctual and steady conduct in the masters, mistresses, or tutors, I propose that there shall be chosen, in each district, by a majority of the whole electors, *forty* persons who shall form a committee of superintendance, *ten* to go out every three months, by rotation, and to be supplied by ten other citizens, who shall also be chosen by an absolute majority of the whole suffrages of the district; these shall be bound to examine once in every month, or as much oftener as they shall think right, all the schools of the district, and make their report to the representative body, and to the district, which report shall be lodged with the register, for public inspection; they shall also audit the accounts of the expenditure attending the public seminaries, and settle the quota of each citizen towards defraying them, every third month, for the ensuing *three months;* as the members of this committee will be immediately interested in their functions, so I propose, that no salary shall attend the execution of them; and to prevent the affairs of the district ever getting into the hands of a junto, I propose, that no citizen, after having served on the committee, shall be again eligible to be chosen for twelve months; they shall also inspect the conduct of the municipal officers, and report thereon.

The qualification of a master or tutor to be, having attained *thirty years,* having resided in the district for *four years,* being father of a family, and having elective franchise.

The qualification for a mistress to be, having attained *twenty-six years,* being a mother, and having resided in the district *seven years.*

The qualification for a member of the committee of inspection to be, having attained *twenty-one years,* having been resident twelve months in the district, having elective franchise, and being father of a family.

I also propose, that no *religious doctrine* whatever shall be taught in the national schools; and that any master, mistress, or tutor may be displaced, on twelve thousand five hundred and one of the electors of the district signifying to the register that he or she has lost their confidence,

I also propose, that twice in every year the scholars of each district shall assemble at some place, to be previously appointed by the committee of superintendance, to celebrate civic games, and other exercises that may be productive of activity and health amongst the youth; on which days also, they shall elect from amongst themselves one of the scholars, who shall deliver *an oration on liberty*, and the benefits accruing from education; which shall be printed and distributed through the Commonwealth, and a copy lodged with the register of the district, signed by the youth who pronounced it.

MILITARY FORCE AND DISCIPLINE.

The introduction of what have been termed *soldiers*, that is to say, men carefully separated from their brother citizens, and exclusively instructed in the art of murdering their fellow-man, has been one of those means of which tyrants have availed themselves to destroy the liberty and independence of man, and subjugate him to that disgraceful state of slavery and oppression, under which we at present see him groaning and languishing in almost every climate; and the evil that has resulted to society from this institution is too glaring and notorious to admit of controversy; yet in a state of association, some kind of defence is absolutely necessary to preserve the citizens from foreign insult, and domestic depredation; now, as every member of the community is equally interested in the preservation of his rights and liberty, and as teaching one man the use of offensive weapons in preference to another, is giving the one a decided superiority and mastery over his fellow-citizen ; and as *corruption* has been enabled, by artful men, to spread its baleful influence over these military automatons, and thus to enslave nations to the arbitrary caprice of individuals, I propose, as a remedy for these evils, and to maintain amongst all the citizens that equality of right, from which alone must flow their respective and collective happiness, and security against oppression—That *every citizen* in the Commonwealth *shall be a soldier, and every soldier a citizen.* For this purpose, I intend that the science of *military tactics* shall form a part of the education of youth ; thus placing all the citizens upon a level in the use of arms, after which, if they suffer their liberty to be wrested from them by ambitious and designing knaves, it will be their own fault, and they deserve only to be slaves. The man, who having the means of preserving his *liberty*, voluntarily gives it up, is unworthy of being a *freemen.*

I therefore propose, that in every district there shall be erected national military schools, into which the youth, after they have attained the age of fourteen, shall be sent for one year more to learn the exercise and duty of a soldier, and defender of himself and his country. The *masters* of these schools to be chosen in the same manner as those of the other seminaries of the Commonwealth, and to be paid in the same manner; the same qualifications to be requisite, and the schools to be under the superintendance of the *committee of forty;* and the expences attending them to be defrayed by the citizens of the district, in the same manner as those incurred by other public schools. I also propose, that one day in every two months, every citizen from the age of fifteen to fifty, shall form himself, with his neighbours, into regiments, and go through the martial exercise and military evolutions: this will prevent their forgetting the great principle of defence, and render them at all times ready and fit to defend their country in case of attack. I also propose, that every citizen who shall have obtained the age of fourteen, shall be furnished by his district, with a firelock and a bayonet, which he shall be bound to keep in complete repair and fit for immediate use, if occasion requires, to defend himself and the Commonwealth.

In cases of public emergency, that is to say, of defence, (for I would propose that the citizens should never enter upon offensive war) the force that shall be deemed necessary by the legislature shall be called out by an equal portion from each district, to be chosen by lot, and without distinction of persons. This force to be paid for their services in such manner, and at such rates as the legislative body shall judge fitting and expedient, and to remain on foot only as long as the public danger shall be declared to exist by the national representation.

Thus all being adequate to the defence of themselves, and of their country, it would be impossible to subjugate, as at present, one part of a nation by another, and, at the same time, the society would be preserved from foreign attack, since it would be, in fact, attacking an hornet's nest to attack a nation of armed men, well disciplined, and whose common and natural interest would consist in supporting and protecting each other. Thus those bloody and cruel wars that have so often depopulated the earth, would receive an effectual check; ambition would not know where to rear its head with any probable chance of success; cruel and blood-thirsty chiefs would be abandoned by an enlightened people, and we should no more have the misfortune to see either an *Alexander* or a *Cæsar;* a *Mahomet* or a *Cortez;* a *Charles the Twelfth* or a *Lewis the Fourteenth;* a *William the Con-*

queror or a *Czar Peter.*—Peace would be restored to the blood drenched earth ; security would reign in the cottage and the city, and men would no longer be liable to have infamous and oppressive measures insolently crammed down their throats with the point of a bayonet, or to be cruelly and wickedly kidnapped ; tyranny would receive its vital blow, and despotism become as obsolete and uncommon as it is now prevalent and fashionable. The necessity of reforming abuses would no where exist, because citizens, instructed in their rights, and rendered capable of defending them, would never suffer a set of wretched and cowardly miscreants to usurp an authority over them not warranted by their nature, nor conducive to the felicity and repose of the people ; spies and informers would get into disuse and disesteem ; gaols would become almost unnecessary, and the science of government really become the art of rendering the Commonwealth happy and flourishing.

PROVISION FOR THE POOR.

Nothing seems more rational than that society should be obliged to provide for all its members, I therefore propose, that in every district there shall be erected *national manufactories* of such articles that every citizen wanting employment may be able to assist. In these manufactories, I propose, none should be admitted unless they produce a voucher from *twelve* of their neighbouring fellow-citizens, to the propriety of their conduct, their industry, and their incapability of procuring employ. To each of those citizens, who shall have past the *age of fifty* without having been enabled to provide for their old age, I propose, that upon production of a certificate, signed by *twelve* of their neighbours, who are citizens, having elective franchise, of their former good conduct, industry, and of their present incapacity, the register of the district shall regularly pay: *four* bushels of wheat per week, or the value thereof at the average market price of the district.

CONSTITUTION.

The first business of the Legislative Body should be to frame a *constitution* upon the sacred "*Rights of Man,*" and all *laws* and *decrees* should be considered as null and of no effect that deviated from the principles of this constitution ; and the proposer, and those concerned, to be at all times answerable to the people for their conduct, a majority of whom shall decide their fate; and in order that the constitution may be such as is convenient and suitable to the people. I propose, that every *seven years* it shall either receive the sanction of a majority of the people; or undergo such alteration as they shall deem necessary; for this purpose a *treble* number of representatives shall be chosen, independent of the ordinary representative body, whose function shall be to examine and revise the constitution, and which function shall cease when that business is completed; their sittings not to exceed *two months* in any case. I propose, that they shall be *paid* in the same manner as the other representatives, and their *qualification* and *mode of election* to be the same.

CALCULATION

Of the Expence of a Government upon the foregoing Plan, for a Population of Ten Millions of Mouths, spread over a Territory comprising fifty Millions of Acres.

Of the above number I suppose there would be three millions of male citizens having elective franchise, that is, who had obtained their eighteenth year; this divided into districts of *twenty-five thousand* each, would make *one hundred and twenty.*

I reckon, for the sake of clearness, the bushel of wheat at six shillings, sterling money.

One hundred and twenty registers, at three bushels of wheat per diem each	£39,420
Three clerks to each register, at 2 bushels of wheat per diem each...........................	78,840
Stationery, &c. for each register's office, suppose one hundred pounds each per annum..........	12,000
Four hundred and eighty deputies, at 4 bushels of wheat per diem each........................	210,240
Travelling expences for each deputy, average at twenty pounds each...........................	9,600
Six clerks to the Committee of Government, at two bushels of wheat per diem each	1,314
Stationery, &c. for the office per annum..........	250
Six clerks to the Committee of Finance, at two bushels of wheat per diem each	1,314
Stationery, &c. for the office, per annum........	250

Six clerks to the Committee of Agriculture, Trade,
  and Provisions, at 2 bushels of wheat per diem
  each.. £1,314
Stationery, &c. for the office, per annum   250
Printing and other contingent expences of the representative body, committees, registers, &c..... 25,000
One hundred and twenty judicial administrators, at
  three bushels of wheat per diem each 89,420
Three clerks to each judicial administrator, at two
  bushels of wheat per diem each 78,840
Stationery, &c. for each office, at £250. per annum 30,000

                                 £528,052

This may be amply provided for by a tax amounting to
one twentieth part of a bushel of wheat, or about *four-pence per acre per annum* on the lands of the Commonwealth, which will produce a sum of *eight hundred and
thirty-three thousand, three hundred and thirty-three
pounds*, and may be collected without any expence, by the
registers of the districts, and will greatly overbalance all
the necessary expences of an *honest* and *rational government*, leaving every year the considerable sum of *three
hundred and five thousand two hundred and eighty-one
pounds*, to be applied to works of *public utility*, and other
casualties, as they may occur.

Taxes, raised by *four-pence* per acre on land....£833,333
Expences of Government 528,052

Balance remaining yearly in the Public Treasury £305,281

Thus every *fourth* year the taxes might be remitted to
all the citizens; on such years I would propose, that they
should celebrate a festival to *economy*.

FINIS.

CPSIA information can be obtained
at www.ICGtesting.com
Printed in the USA
BVHW04*1049170918
527708BV00015B/2038/P

9 780484 401029